Broken With Power

Spoken Word/ Poetry

Written by: Brandi Beasley

Known by many as Brandi Agape

Psalm 91:1

He that dwelleth in the secret place of the Most High shall abide under the shadow of the Almighty.

Who am I?

The story of my life is one of complexity. Hate, abuse, rejection and abandonment gravitated to me. I was a captive to foster homes, group homes, hospitals, a children's home and an academy. Eventually I found myself a victim of the streets of New Orleans as a teen. The story goes on and on.. I endured so much pain in my life, that I had no choice, but to allow God to turn it into love.

Agape and God Bless You,
Brandi Beasley, (*Brandi Agape)*

"The Secret Place of the Most High"

There is a place I go, that is in side of God
A place I go where the enemy can't see
A place where darkness can't be seen
A place that contradicts every word the devil has ever spoken
A place of no tears
A place of no fears
A place of restoration and of rest
A place of peace that passes all understanding
A place where even the rivers worship the LORD
A place where rainbows cover my being
A place where I can feel free to be me
A place where the Word He has put in my heart unfolds
A place where my Faith in Him can't be controlled
A place where nothing can express how great His Love is for me
And how he longs to reveal Himself unto me
And how even the smile on His face imparts virtue in me
And where His very Presence comforts my revelation knowledge
A place where things grow but don't die
A place where there is no past to leave behind
A place where I have no flesh to go through changes
A place where there are no young or old ages
A place where I don't have to travail
A place where there is no thought of the devil or hell
A place where music is not sound
A place where I walk but not on a ground
A place where I can't be rejected
A place where feelings are not spoken in words
A place where His total focus is on me
A place that never changes
"The Secret Place of The Most High"

To God Be the Glory

June 15, 2004

"Holy Spirit I Call Thee"

Holy Spirit I call thee
I need thee
I thirst for thee
Let your presence consume me
My travail has formed the keys to
Open the windows of Heaven
Holy Spirit I call thee to come unto me
I starve for the presence of the Most High
My soul rest at the Gates of His mind
Holy Spirit I wait on thee
Precious Holy Spirit I yearn for thee
I want to feel you Holy Spirit
I need to hear you calling me
I need to feel you drawing me
I need you to hide me under His wings
I need you to guide me
Share the secrets of my own heart with me
I need you to teach me
I need you God speed
I need you to birth forth The Fathers seed
I need you to keep me on the road to eternity
I need thee Oh
I need thee..
Every hour
I need thee
To consume me
Commune with me
Usher me into His divine presence
Keep Me
Holy Spirit I Call Thee

June 30, 2005 1:15 am

He Loves Me"

Though sometime my pain tries to take over
I know in my heart
God is the eternal beholder
His love embraces me
Causing me to shine
Like the..
Morning star..
He loves me..
Bringing me food from afar
He is the fountain of my soul
He is my eyes when I can't see
He is the one who gently washed and set my mind free
Having mercy on me
He calls me a daughter in Zion
He loves me

Saturday, February 26, 2005

"Glory"

Eagles with rainbow wings soar through the sky
Leaving trails of diamond dust
The reflection from the sunshine
Radiates off of the echoes of travail from the sound of the Children of God
The repentance of man's heart..
The separation of brokenness between the spirit and the soul..
The birth of a child..
The cry of the Martyrs..
The transition of those dead in Christ..
It ignites the flame in the heart of the Chosen
It gives hope and strength to the weary
It reveals the hidden mysteries of God, making way for His wisdom

"Liberty"

My spirit tells of thee
And your sweet peace of liberty
As my souls stands to solute the "Omni Present Flag" of my life
I inhale the Glory that saturates eternity
Holy.. Holy.. Holy.. Holy..
Is He..
Whose name is above ALL names
Empty.. I lay prostrate on the threshing floor
My spirit laments..
My soul repents..
I stand for righteousness
I stand for purity
I stand for the Word of God
I stand to say to all who has an ear to hear
Consecrate yourself
Humble yourself
Under the hand of the almighty God

Thursday, August 2, 2004

"Meditation"

My curiosity of love journeys His divine presence
As I sit and await the Holy Spirit to consume my impatience
I cast down every wicked imagination that interferes with my destination
Preparing my spirit to be absent from the flesh
And present with God
Not knowing what to expect
I whisper to my soul
Peace be still

August 2004

"I Shall"

I Shall
Take up my bed and walk in peace
Come at the lift of the Kings hand
Let my eyes be on the field that I will reap
Lay at His feet at midnight and not move until He commands
Be as a crown unto the Lord
Trained up in the way I should go
Be as a cold snow in the time of harvest
Enter into the door of the sheepfold
I shall not be faithless but believe
Nor put a limit on the power of God
Not be weary in well doing
I'll trust in the LORD with all my heart
Understanding that a just man falls
But gets back up again
I shall by no means ever forget
That Jesus is my husband and my best friend

Monday, August 30, 2004

"Peculiar"

Rivers of water run down my face
Your Word pumps through my heart into my soul
I wail at your feet
I am a stranger in the earth
Incline my heart unto your holiness
I have turned unto thee
My hope is in thy Word
I have girded myself with destiny

2004

"Who Are You?"

Who Are You?
That even the rivers worship you
To whom the trees lift up their branches in praise
Even to you the wind cries Hoooo lyyyy
Who Are You?
That created Jesus and the Holy Ghost
That created me in your image
Then gave me a body and a soul
Who Are You?
That is
Love
Joy
Peace
Longsuffering
Gentleness
Goodness
Faith
Meekness
Temperance
Who Are You?
That taught me to walk in the spirit
Live in the Spirit
To hunger and thirst after righteousness
Who Are You?
That everything that grows looks up to you
That made the sky red but it looks blue
That made the beginning and eternity to

Who Are You?

Sunday, May 29, 2005
6:30pm

"Yes I Do See Him"

Diverse wicked imaginations disperse
At even the thought of Him who knew me before birth
Who proclaimed my victory and gave me self worth
Who purged me with hyssop
The one who sprinkled in my spirit frankincense and myrrh
Yes
I am that head and not the tail
I was created to do the will of the Most High
Whose simple knowledge confuses the bible scholars minds
Just His very presence makes demons run and hide
In this broken down temple He chose to abide
And He's renovating
I Do See
The vision that He has placed before my spirit
I have eyes to look upon what even the priest can't see
It's obedience that gives me love, joy, hope and peace
His Love hurts so good
It's breaking me down into humility
Bringing the HIM out of me
Exposing the enemy that tries to confuse who I be
HIM
Who's name is Jehovah
And there is no other greater
The annihilator of the wicked
Who is my strength
Who is everlasting
Who is refreshing to my soul
Him who by the world is not known
Who allowed His Sons blood to be shed
So that we can go home
And not be left to burn in the fire alone
Yes I Do See Him

Monday, June 14, 2004

"Unlimited Love"

My God..
My Savior..
My opportunity to express His unlimited Love
That grips my soul like a hand in a glove
The same love that cast satan from heaven to his grave
My Love..
My Help..
My Peace..
My Mercy..
My Grace..
My understanding of purity and holiness
My deliverance from hurt, pain and loneliness
He who covered me with His rod
When I was searching for my Brokenness
Misunderstood by man
I understood that
The fear of the LORD is the beginning of wisdom
And it helped me to know that
Before He formed me in my mother's womb
I was Blessed..
And Chosen..
To defeat the enemy..
Chosen to travail..
Until I was wrapped in His garment like a cocoon
The same cocoon that formed my wings
Enabling me to mount my wings and fly like an eagle
That same cocoon prepared me to soar through the nations

Wednesday, May 4, 2005

"Purification"

The burning
The Purification
The release of utterance
Consecration
Emptiness
Brokenness
Contrite tears
From the sword of a warrior
Separation
Help that comes from chastening
Elevation that comes from yearning
The wisdom of fear
Hearing spiritual ears
Can you hear it?
The flow of living water
Release it
Can't You See?
Holy
Pure
Humble
Meek
The Salvation of the LORD Is
Honey so sweet
The Joy of love
Perfect yet unique
Hunger from the crown of the head, to the sole of the feet
A baby that was birthed out of righteousness
An ant that carries the extra weight, that extra mile
The smile that is released from the Heart of God
To the soul of His remnant

Tuesday, June 28, 2005, 11:47pm

"I Have Purposed In My Heart"

I have purposed in my heart to please you
I have purposed in my heart to be broken
I have purposed in my heart to get more of you
I have purposed in my heart to become you
To think like you
To See like you
To walk like you
To talk like you
To hear like you
To obey you
To bring peace like you
To have a heart pure and true
To see others like you do
To be controlled by you
To be used by you
To speak life like you
To be a good wife to you
LORD God Almighty I give my life to you
Because I love you
I have purposed in my heart to please you

Thursday, June 30, 2005, 12:43pm

"You Are"

A life time of Smiles
The shoulder that dries up my tears
You are my best friend
When my world falls apart, your arms are opened
Over and over again
Only God knows how your love so sweet still says hello
And how yesterday still gives a futile hand wave
My Lord.. My Savior.. I'm yours
In time that will never end
You made my Yesterdays turn into Joyful days
Our love is eternal

"Agape"

Attempting to concentrate on my purpose
I embark on the word LOVE
In which my heart has put so much emphasis on
It cradles my Life with significance
It lures my soul in with hope and longevity
It overcomes every battle in my mind
It persecutes the enemy with pure authority
It astonishes me
Yes.. LOVE astonishes me
Who is like unto LOVE?

Saturday, March 19, 2011, written in the am

"Tears of Oil"

Through my eyes
Oil falls like tear drops
When I embrace your presence
The things that seem distant are close
The things that seem close are distant
Tears of Joy I call them
The Oil of Joy I call it
My pleasure..
I say in my heart..
To worship your eternal love..

Love

Joy

Peace

And Hope..
My worship walks through

Depression

Hurt

And Rejection..
My soul yearns for your purity
My tears and worship are in love with you
Almighty God..
My worship loves you because you embrace it..
My tears love you because they've never hit the floor..
Even when my face was yet at your feet
They were caught by your presence..

Treasured

Nurtured

Prepared for eternity..
Being called in your heavenly language
"Tears of Oil"

Monday, November 29, 2004

"Oh Ye of Little Faith"

I know you hurt
I see your tears
I see your fears
Oh ye of little faith
I know the plans I have for you
To make you, to break you
To be intimate with you
To unfold my mysteries unto you
To teach you to embrace my Manifold Wisdom..
I'm calling you to come to me
I want to show you my face
Come seek me
I can see that you hunger for me
Oh ye of little faith
I know you hurt
I see your tears
I see your fears
Oh ye of little faith
I know the plans I have for you
To make you, to break you
To be intimate with you
To unfold my mysteries unto you
To teach you to embrace my Manifold Wisdom..
Trust in me
Worship me
Come to me
Oh ye of little faith

Saturday, February 26 2005, 9:45am

"The Road to My Destiny"

Thou art the road to my destiny
My soul will sing unto thee
You found the greatness that was hid by my weariness
I am a wonder unto many
They say in their heart
There is no help for me in you.. Oh God
By thee, have I been kept from the womb
For thou art my hope, O Lord God
Thou art my strong refuge
Let me never be put to confusion
Let me never wear the face of shame
Let your love be my armor
And your mercy be my strength
Let your glory decrease me
And you're anointing tear down walls that have been sent to seclude and
destroy me
Let me escape the waters that come to drown me
Let me trust only in righteousness
Let me live for you
Let me become you
I want to see what you see
Because...
Thou art the road to my destiny

"Soul"

As the beauty from a misty rain sits on the face of a magnolia
The Lords train fills the Kingdom floors
A key is put into a lock and many doors fly open
A Christian's face embraces the concrete before the LORD
As travail is to persecution
Every knee shall bow and every tongue shall confess
Time will never end
The flames in hell will never rest
As the Anointing destroys the yoke
The Spirit is master over the flesh
As martyrs await the day of the LORD
A walking dead man has no spiritual regrets

Wednesday, July 2, 2003, 12:56pm

"Adonijah"

A trail of tears rest upon the Lords train
As He walks the kingdom floors
Cast away by man
I lay at the sole of His feet
Renouncing hurt...
I declare there is no room left in me any more
He picks up my broken soul
And kisses me with His eyes...
I've never had a kiss that made me whole
A kiss that made me white as snow
That made my skin glow
That put my flesh under control
That made that empty space I embraced
Overflow...
With...
Rivers of living water...
My spirit sings...
Adonijah...the Lord is my master
The strength of my walls
Father of the dew
The land of my morning...
Almon Amad...Hidden people of witness
That hide under His radiant wings
We are...
Ammishaddai... The people of the Almighty
And He who is with us is
Faithful and True...
Holy is He...
Whose presence rest upon...
His remnant...
His coming is near...
I become silent
Resting in His presence
His Love lifts me
Enabling me to stand
we begin to walk...
And I say in my heart...
Adonijah...The Lord is my master

January 27, 2005

"Control"

Though my soul burns with imitation desires
Lord I read in your Word that you're not a man that you should be a liar
You told me that there are some things that my flesh just cannot comprehend
That is why the flesh rebels against the spirit man
And in my soul, I am sometimes so confused
Because in my past I was so used and abused
You taught me to make my spirit master over my soul
That way my flesh will be under your control
Although some things are so hard to let go
I know that unless my soul surrenders
Spiritually there are place that I just can't go

Wednesday, February 9, 2005
9:12am

"Yearning"

Your presence consumes me with inspiration
I yearn for your intimacy
I yearn for your chastisement
I yearn for the beauty of your holiness
Jehovah! Your presence consumes me

Thursday, February 15, 2007 9:00am

"Only God Knows"

Only God Knows...
How eternity never has an end
The pain when one loses a brother, child, spouse or friend
Only God knows
The Joy that comes from sadness
The peace that comes from understanding
The binding and separating..
Of the spirit, body and soul
Only God knows
The hate that dwells in selfishness
The Victory in selflessness
What true perfection is..
Only God knows
His hope for tomorrow
The redemption needed for this life..
That we've borrowed
How we will be..
Changed tomorrow
When this world will pass away
The secret of night and day
Who will go and who will stay
The pain from the unquenched flames
The Glory resting upon the Saints
The second that He will return
On His Coming Day
Only God Knows

"I Will Wait and Fear Not"

(Inspired by Psalm 27)

LORD you are my light and my salvation, the strength of my life
Whom shall I fear?
He who rides upon the golden horse in my night
Of Whom shall I be afraid?
When people speak, gathering against me, they shall stumble and fall
When they have come to war against me, they shall be defeated by the
brazen alter
Because..
When you said, "Seek my face"
My heart said
Your face LORD will I seek
I desire to dwell in your house LORD, more than anything
To behold your beauty and enquire in your temple
All the days of my life..
I will offer in your tabernacle, sacrifices of Joy
I will sing.. I will honor you.. I will worship you..
Oh God
When I cry with my voice
You have mercy on me
You are my help and do not hide your face from me
You are teaching me your ways
You are leading me on a plain path
You have never left me nor forsaken me
And because the vision you have put before me,
I did not faint..
And because of your goodness and you being my hope
The cup I did drink
And because you are the LORD of the living
I will wait..
I will wait on you LORD
I will be of good courage..
I know you will strengthen me..
I will wait on you LORD..
"I Will Wait and Fear Not"

Saturday, January 29, 2005, 12:00pm

"Yesterday, Today, Tomorrow"

Yesterday, Today, Tomorrow
Consecration, Holiness, Spiritual Peace
Lifestyles, Worldly trends, unexplained self defeat
Pressing, pressing, pressing
Anointing destroying every yoke
Cigarettes choking the Holy Ghost
Lying, Killing, Stealing
Praying, Weeping, Travailing
Laying at the soul of the LORDS feet
Yesterday, Today, Tomorrow
Consecration, Holiness, Spiritual Peace
Lifestyles, Worldly trends, unexplained self defeat
Pressing, pressing, pressing
Anointing destroying every yoke
Cigarettes choking the Holy Ghost
Lying, Killing, Stealing
Praying, Weeping, Travailing
Laying at the soul of the LORDS feet
What would you do if the Lord returned today?
What would you do?
What would you say?
What price did you pay to allow that Holy Ghost to have his way?
What did you lose?
What did you gain?
By sometimes feeling pain
By sometimes feeling things that you can't even explain?
Tears pouring down like rain
Do you seek worldly pleasure or eternal gain?
Yesterday, Today, Tomorrow
Consecration, Holiness, Spiritual Peace
Lifestyles, Worldly trends, unexplained self defeat
Pressing, pressing, pressing
Anointing destroying every yoke
Cigarettes choking the Holy Ghost
Lying, Killing, Stealing
Praying, Weeping, Travailing
Laying at the sole of the LORDS feet

"Eternity"

Pure Gold Street as if it were transparent glass
No moon
No sun
No Night
No Day
God's glory the Lamb does shine
The saints shall walk in it
The kings of the earth do bring their glory and honor into it
Being part of that crystal clear sea
That will stand before the throne of the Lamb of God
They who are called to eternity
Being seen by God without spot or blemish
The same
In whom the Lord says well done my good and faithful servant
Even before the foundations of the world
Those who were written in the Lambs Book of Life from the beginning
Those who were Chosen to be the Sons and daughters of God
And heirs of His power and authority before the womb
Those same ones who have no room for iniquity
Because the light in them does shine
All tears and hurt
Will be left behind
All hunger and thirst
Will be left behind
All disease and sickness of all kind
Will be left behind
No flesh, No death, No travail
No weeping, No Wail
Nor male, Nor female
No hospital walls or jail cells
And no deformities
Only God's image
And eternal purpose
From the Beginning

Monday, May 23, 2005

Broken With Power

1 Corinthians 15:31

1 Corinthians 5:17

1 Peter 2:24

2 Corinthians 4:8

1 Corinthians

2 Corinthians 3:3

Romans 8

Colossians

1 Peter 4:1-11

Philippians 1:21

Made in the USA
Middletown, DE
03 March 2024

50189581R00017